ROLLERCOASTERS & BEDSHEETS

AN ANTHOLOGY OF SEX IN MINUTES

Edited by
Charlene Shepherdson and Muslim Sahib

Pillow Book Media.

ISBN-978-981-09-7460-2

Typeset by diacriTech Ptv Ltd
Cover design and illustrations by Illi Syaznie

Content Page

Editors' Preface

The taboo of being associated with sex and erotica is the main motivation behind *Rollercoasters & Bedsheets*. During the open call, the most frequent question posed by contributors was, "Can I submit my poems under a pseudonym?" and our task here is to destigmatise the conversations around this topic. Sex in the media is often portrayed as a deed done quick and dirty, and the real-life issues around communication, power play and consent are often unaddressed.

The realm of sex and relations is a rollercoaster of passion, emotions, and lust. More often than not, we do not possess the vocabulary to articulate these experiences. *Rollercoasters & Bedsheets* delves into these frenzied territories and takes one on an emotional pilgrimage to explore the notion of self-identity, the experimentation between truth and fantasy, and the examination of hidden boundaries.

The idea of using poetry as a means to explore sex and erotica allows the conversation to grow organically. What is often touted as popular literature on BDSM and alternative sex lifestyles are fraught with misconceptions. The poems featured in this anthology are selected for the diversity of views that they represent. We hope that these insightful pieces will add on to existing discussions and provide opportunities for discourse.

Embark on your own sexual journey within this safe space—be it on, under, or between your bedsheets. Let us learn to articulate our desires, so that we can be empowered and comfortable in our own skin.

Acknowledgements

The editors would like to thank the following people who have been instrumental in producing this anthology:

Pillow Book Media Pte. Ltd. for their assistance from conception to print. You saw the value in our proposition before getting down to the intimate details.

Our contributors for their honest and open contributions. You have been amazing poets and collaborators during the editing process.

You, our reader, for getting into bed with us and listening to our stories.

Rollercoasters

You always had to force me

To

Take

The ride

To ponder

The long wait

The long climb

The long screams

To fantasise firmament

Till my legs utterly succumb

To kinetic Stockholm syndrome

Your unrelenting quest for a thrill

Muslim Sahib

One

The first time I felt

iced metal on skin—such bliss,

this coming of age

Photograph

All I could think of that night: rain
punishing our meager coats, two people
not disillusioned enough
to be strangers, but conveniently
prepared as friends, the way a child
has everything to fear and
yet fears nothing, how my
father slept in the hotel two blocks
away, and how I gave myself
to another unsympathetic body
and suspected nothing.

Jerrold Yam

Prayers to Harem

Master bed in the hive hall
Hung masks on the filthy wall
Harem full of half dressed
Living dead dolls

Jungle fever delirium
Fumes and alcohol
Vines, thick and veined
Growling mating calls
Suspension ropes
Weights and hooks
and zentai suits

Predator pounces prey

Dirty debutantes
coiling at my feet
Bodies painted,
cosplayed and crawling:

        Hello pussy suits
        Half fish girls with breast clamps
        (we're not in Kansas anymore)
        "O, you lion! Beastial king!"
        Straitjackets and straps
        Aphrodisiac love potions

See!
My comatose bride
Death pose
Hands on chest with bloodied rose
(Waiting for Gonad,
for necromantic kiss)

HOWL
The wolf rides the red haired hooded one,
stark naked in stark darkness:
"The best minds of my generation fuck beauties like beasts."
"Grandfather! You have such big teeth!"

A procession of princesses:

> Elsa teased with ice on labia
> Poca, colonised by white men
> Cinderella fondling feet
> Snow White flesh and happy endings
> for six bearded men and a dope fiend

But there is only one queen.
Leather spiked
Brute force of pleasure

This is the garden of earthly delights
A pandemonium passion of lash and nail
Blood and water and erotic pain
Bathtubs of soap and sin

They offer me the milk of Nut*,
kneel and pray to their goat headed horned god

on the Master bed,

in the heart of

harem hall.

Irving Paul Pereira

*Nut is the goddess of the sky in the Ennead of ancient Egyptian religion. She was seen as a star-covered nude woman arching over the earth.

Lunar

Once a year, soft skin peels back to
reveal the feathered intimacy of fragile blossoms as
children laugh and fondle their innocence under

the watchful gaze of fathers and mothers long
past their own curiosity. The buds rupture, aptly surrounded
by the copious colour of graduating virginity, and

little boys and girls unknowingly ripen with
accidentally ingested stems and soft giggles as
willow branches brush against necks and

palms, wide open like their enkindled eyes. In these
tender days, naivety and discovery coalesce as
nascent sight and touch are fulfilled.

Noses take in the salty tang of simmering abalone and tongues
entwine the pleated creases of these yonic morsels, regardless
of undiscovered inclinations.

Ignatius Tan

Sorry, Tommy

For the record, I was sober.

I started dancing with you to a piano song
I don't remember, and when I got bored, you
spoke to Alex: you were both talking about
sexuality. He said later, it was something
about your song about wanting to be tied up
that got to him, the same song I thought
sounded pretentious, or maybe I'd never
wanted to think of you that way. I mean,
when you told him you were open to
'experimentation', I thought it was because
you thought that was the cool thing to say.

At some point, I guess your lips found mine.
Our hands slid over one another's shoulders
as we closed our eyes. As I was about
to put it all down to another night
of scientific inevitability,
a new hand found its way up my waist.

Then you were shirtless on your back
between me and Alex—two lions sharing their quarry.

You looked so gorgeous with your face
disappearing into his, I almost said sorry
for misjudging you, for lying that I liked your music,
so I traced the message on your belly with my fingertips
and the edge of my tongue, that part that they say
best detects sweetness.

At sunrise, Alex made you come in his mouth
just before he slipped away. I woke to your moan,
you told me how you had never really felt anything
that wonderful before, asked me how I figured out

I was bisexual, and as we stared
at one another's naked bodies
in the sunshine, I stopped seeing you
as a try-too-hard naïve little boy,
not just a nervous, stumbling, un-intimidating
new kid who just wanted to be smiled at,
like the one I buried years ago.

But as a person
lying in the same spot in the sun as me,
a kid who, like me, just wanted to scream
out from the window:
'OMG I JUST HAD MY FIRST THREESOME!'

Just a really cool kid
doing an impression
of an uncool kid
doing an impression
of that cool kid
that we will never admit
we think we are
deep down inside.

Stephanie Chan

As Bleak as your Skype Connection

We try to slow down every time,
delay the time taken from getting in
front of the camera to ripping off our clothes.
Punctuate the silence with "How are you?" and
"What did you do today?"
Our record is ten minutes.

My parents have gone to sleep,
and yours, not yet awake.
My body is illuminated by the miserable fluorescent light
and yours by the rays of the early morning sun.

The computer fan is louder than either of us.
When small talk ends,
the rustling and removal of clothes begin.

We stay still, naked for a moment,
before you want me to tell you what to do.
"Take out your birthday present, baby,
but don't take off that chastity cage."
You'll be vulnerable so I try to be firm.
"Bend over and show yourself to me, baby."
You bring the pink bit of vibrating plastic
between your cheeks
and pretend it's me.

We touch each other through the screen,
pressing through to the other side
as reality and the interwebs bend and warp
against our fingertips.
Skype flickers dangerously every five minutes,
your internet connection almost gives way.
"Take it off, baby, I'll let you touch yourself."

The fingers in me feel too familiar.
I try to pretend they're yours.

We look unhinged.

Perfectly in sync,
we burn together, 13 time zones apart.
Hold back our moans.
Stop ourselves before we scream.

Why are you so quiet, baby?

Look up.
Look up.

Please don't cry.

"I love you," you say.
I hear "I'll wait for you".

I nod.
I say goodbye.

Drima Chakraborty

Coming Out

Dear recent explosion of feminist friends,

There is something I need to tell you. I sometimes feel like a walking Tumblr post, #YourSexLifeIsProblematic. Maybe I've reclaimed my *shame shame* about my body, my embarrassment burning on a different set of cheeks where I'm going to engulf the flames with fetish.

Sorry, but I've extinguished all my apologies, handcuffed my anxiety, spread-eagled and vibrating with various devices. Sometimes, I find comfort in being collared, rolling over, and playing dead. Instead of hitting rock-bottom—I'd rather get my bottom hit.

I know you probably won't be too accepting of this, but I think you need to know that I find the idea of verbal vitriol slightly amusing. I find the idea of pejoratives in power play slightly arousing. Maybe I'm being complicit in my oppression while finding liberation on a leash.

So, as part of our aftercare, when you protest my objectification with, "I object!", I will lovingly stroke you on your harness and say, "No. You human."

Marylyn Tan

Aftermath

I would lie on my back—behind me
wood or cloth or another's pulsating flesh—
scrutinising what I have worked on
as a mother anxiously inspects her newborn,
my prize and art losing fluidity
to the sterile air, caking
in tiny rivulets
across my arm and chest. Sometimes,
in the damp of a locked room,
I would press my tongue to
its strange viscosity, like a child
licking ice-cream that has strayed
to his elbows, and be comforted by
how this cannot be too different
from eating one's children,
except that denial of life is more
benevolent than its fulfillment. If I have
enough courage, I could see
all the world's men
naked and straining after their
own myopic pleasures, how strangely
self-sufficient the male body! There
should not be room for intention
or surprise. When a baby
has been woven, it is not allowed
back to the braided
sanctum of its mother, harmless
and diligent, to unstitch
its only chance at death.

Jerrold Yam

gears warm up, motors purr,

knees interlock under

rising ombre sheets

Porn

Executive

Boss, office work is
not drudgery when I get
hard from 9 to 5.

Teabagging

Yes, steep your essence
in my mouth. I am your cup;
I am your water.

Bareback

Praise the body's pure
perfection. Worship truly
without protection.

Ladyboy

Ladies and gents, here's
our one-time offer: get two
for the price of one.

Bukkake

Dear dozen, my face
is your canvas: splashes of
pearlescent Pollock.

Rodrigo Dela Peña, Jr.

Meat

Eating *bak chor mee** with an executive;
he slurps up a pork liver and tells me that
he has made plans to explore my body.
I do not ponder this threat for long,
distracted instead by the steaming broth
bobbing with soft, round bribes.
Both eyes closed, I whisper a confused cry;

when I see him again, it will be
Oscar-winning smiles and banal demands—

but we start small.
He buys me a plate of innards
like it is some special thing.

It is tantalising.

Keith Tong

*Bak Chor Mee is a Chinese mincemeat noodle dish.

Ego

Loneliness tugs at ego's shaft
and self-pity pulls the skin back up
and over its head until it doesn't recognise
itself anymore, lost in its own darkness.

Repeated enough, this pendulum motion
makes ego blush
with the blood of pride rising
to its rosy tip.

Narcissism eventually
erupts into a stream of
self-congratulatory platitudes and burns
guilt into the back of mind, saving it for later

when ego collapses and cowers
under the shadow of its former
colossal self.

See Wern Hao

Daredevil

I don't know how to tie ropes,
I tried out for Girl Guides
then joined Drama because

could you imagine me
singing songs around a campfire
but I want to sing for you.

So loud that the neighbours
break down our doors, tell us to keep it down
because sex this noisy
borders on public indecency.

But know that I'll never leave you
hanging. Put a collar on my neck so
you'll always have a hold on me.

Hold my chain like a balloon
as I float higher and higher.
Keep me tethered to you
so I don't drift away.

I daydream about watching TV with you,
Matt Murdock beating up some other baddie
but we won't know who he's fighting
because it's a bit hard to tell with
my tongue down your throat.

You're hard.

I'm the devil, do you dare?
Because I don't.

Every time you're next to me,
I want to kiss you.
But I don't.

Drima Chakraborty

Venom

My tongue
Traces the edge
Her lips
Soft
Inviting

My tongue
Flicks the silver studs
Snakebites
My poison
Healing

Nickie Jamison

8 Truths and 1 Lie

1. "I love it when you do that."
An iambic finger.
Unstressed. Stressed. Unstressed. Stressed.
She is poetry in motion.
A throbbing current to get lost in.

2. "You are so big."
Manhandles a thing so concrete,
you know by the way nerves tingle at its reach.
So delicate, the true start and end
of sex is a dream one misstep away.

3. "This is my first time."
Averting eyes.
A parting invitation.
She smiles because she knows
you want it.
To know her beginning.
To have ownership of her experience.
When did she start counting?

4. "Don't stop!"
Her eyes are squeezed shut.

5. "Oh God, yes!"
Her mouth is a melted marshmallow.
So hot.
So wet.

6. "Harder. Harder. Harder."
Atoms speaking the language of fusion.
You are planets in collision.
This must be how lights kiss.

7. "I love you. I love you. I love you."
Dough kneaded by hand.
Rising in heat.
Her words are the scent of freshly baked bread.

8. "I'm coming!"
You spill into her.
She is the holy grail,
meant to give and take life.

9. "Fuck. You came all over my bed!"
You see her now.
Hair strewn across her shoulders like unkempt seaweed.
Cheeks blushing like a Chinese firecracker.
Her eyes glinting from irresistible frustration.
Tainted.
Strong.
Human.
You fall into her lips
amidst flailing limbs.
A good place to drop anchor.

Jedidiah Huang

Three.

rollercoasters and bedsheets

freefall into a trail of intimates

Sexiest Times of the Day

0300
All good sex inevitably ends here
after inevitably beginning at 0000.
This is a time of weighted sighs.
Of pliable skin.
Slow grazing fingertips.
Heart-to-heart-wordless-conversation.
This is breathing easy.

0700
You try to wake up a minute earlier.
It is a silent race to sneak out of bed before the other wakes.
Brush your teeth,
wash the "essential parts",
before gently dropping back into bed.
Her hair is a mess.
Her eyes puffy from sex.
Her lips are ajar.
You kiss her into the morning.
You know she finds it unfair,
only you get to see her in full morning glory.
Wake up earlier next time.

1030
You are stuck behind a desk.
You are filling paperwork you don't believe in.
You can't help but think about the morning's goodbye kiss.
This is the time of hangovers.
The droopy eyes after a dream.
You think,
maybe
if you close your eyes,
the dream will come back.
The files remain spread eagle on your desk.

1500
This is 1030,
with extra biryani* from lunch and an inbox-full of work

All in all, too much work for the rest of the day,
and too much day for you to leave.
Your phone vibrates,
"Can't wait to see you later! ;)"
This is true torture.

1900
It's been a long day.
You stumble through the door
into her scent
of ginger and soya sauce.
Good foreplay always begins with food.
She greets you, spatula still in hand,
running shorts and oversized shirt.
You have lost the race to make dinner.

2100
Her head has tucked neatly into your neck.
The news drones on.

2115
A stray hand sinks between her thighs.
Cue hot make out session.

2359
You tug at the condom wrapper with your teeth.
She waits thirty seconds
before rolling her eyes and snatching it from your mouth.
I swear I almost had it.

0000
All good sex inevitably begins here.

Jedidiah Huang

*Biryani is an Indian rice dish.

Predictive Text

Your shoes will be the first to go.

Then your earrings, will be remov[enter]
your necklace, unclasped

and your lingerie, dropped
followed by your dre[enter].

Though we both know
this thirst will remain unquenc[enter]

My eyes will still dri[enter] you
by the mouthful.

So crushed mout[enter]
and stifled gas[enter].

My tongue will li[enter] the light off
the arch of your ba[enter], the curves of your feet.

So quickened heartbe[enter]
curled toes on wrink[enter] sheets.

Let me meand[enter] over the vastness
of skin left undev[enter] still.

I will show you how wetn[enter]
and warmth are only synonyms

We will do what we have to do
not to wake the neighb[enter]

I will do what I have to do
not to stop until you beg me to

[enter]

Sheena Baharudin

Burden

You told me that you'd never done this before,
but the smile on your face makes this a lie,
we lie, and lay together, and we can't close
the space between us with just a touch.

There's no wrong or right in this world,
you told me once, only shades of grey.
You didn't mean the book. There
wasn't a trick you didn't already know.

No answers at the bottom of a bottle.
Nothing to offer but sad smiles and gentle encouragement.
When I see you in the halls you look at your shoes
but alone in the dark, air thick with crickets
and the smell of incense, you're always looking up.

Maybe this was a bad idea.
Maybe we all get what we deserve.
If that was true, why am I here?

With desert sand in my veins,
and sound of shells, my lullaby.
You're alone, heavy chest,

still in that old trailer,
with my name on your lips
and my burden at your breast.

Jason Purdy

Almost like Kissing

The way you eat a river snail,
she says, is to put the shell to
your mouth, and your tongue

over half the opening.
Blow in hard then
inhale, quickly

and the body will slide
into your mouth. She says,
it's almost like kissing.

> Consider the bowl of steaming black shells in front of you,
> freshly- picked from the banks of Sungei Rejang.
>
> Consider all the stories you could tell about the things
> they made you eat in your two weeks in the rainforest.
>
> Consider the way she is watching you right now, which you
> would tell others about, if you could only describe it.

Close your eyes. Mould your lips
around the opening like a whistle: the
sharp edge digs into your tongue, grey

snail juice trails down your arm. Try to
ignore the muddy taste of the single
grey muscle as it goes in your mouth.

Swallow it like all the stories she's been
telling you, steamed in myths and half-
truths you haven't begun to pull apart.

> She asks you, *how*?
> When the look on your face tells her all, consider her raised
> eyebrow and the careful tone of that one syllable.

Stephanie Chan

I Slip a Cloth from You

Beneath the blankets,
we whispered our lives to each other.
Soft sentences, rough truths
that lie across our ears, and
dampen the sweat on our brows.
I breathe in your morning breath,
quiet and slow, sink deeper
into your safety scent.
A skin net to twine our limbs, we wrap
it around us and twitch the nerves
of our cross-haired existence.
Those times with you under
the sheets, make sleep irrelevant.
Belief that our demons would
pull the covers off our bodies,
reveal our nakedness for all to see.
If only you made it easier for me; abandoned
me without the hope of touch. Sure
lips left me with only the cool imprint
of your body on the bed.

There is no succour,
just insatiability of your sex.
Is there a next?
I will be the only one
to slip a cloth from you.
Desire does this to you,
drives you to the brink,
leaves you numb at the edge.
But I obsess;
hair, lips, hand and leg,
that you would not leave me
one day
begging, to let me go and
let you in.
The many wonders of our sin.

Christopher Fok

For Ice Cream

I should have found it odd,
I suppose, that driving past
a glowing Baskin Robbins
would make me think of you.

But now I have to admit
I want nothing more
than to use the tip
of my tongue like a little
pink plastic spoon
as I sample
the multifarious flavors of you.

From Belly Button Swirl
to Neckline Divine,
I will savor slowly
your every ounce,

melt you between my lips
as I explore the subtle
smoothness of your
chocolate-caramel-coffee
Neapolitan skin.

After much intentional indecisiveness,
to taste and re-taste,
I will finally choose my favorite
and reach for your neck—
the sugar cone I cannot wait to nibble on,
which holds the sweet, round
perfect round scoop of your mouth.

I'll do everything I can
not to let one drop
go unappreciated or unadulterated,
even lick you
from my fingertips.

And together you and I will indulge
in the childish fun of making a mess
and cleaning it up—as if our eyes
were full of hot summer days
and there isn't a rocky road
in sight.

KJ Ink

Neon Angels

In the plumes

of dry ice,

pulsing lights are

metronomes for hips.

Spinning in neon,

pumping fists persuade heaving bosoms

like sirens beckon sailors to

crash on rocks.

From rough winds,

they flounder in the dark waters,

feeling limbs

and emptying frustrations.

Pamela Ng

Post Coital Confession

Our words tumbled from our mouths
as if to fill a side bowl of cheap bar snacks.

We ordered another round of absinthe shots
(blue and minty and rather pleasant, wasn't it?
Definitely not the stuff that consumed Mr. Wilde).

You spoke of the woman and the man sitting across from her.
"He wants to fuck her," you said. You always had a
flair for languages—Hindi, Gurmukhi, Latin and Body.

We stumbled home in a taxi, as is customary.
The clothes came off faster than you could
say, "I want to fuck you".

Fucking was what we did,
rough and raw as you liked.

I didn't mention it but somewhere
between moist heavy breaths,
your tongue in my ear and
the words you uttered so tenderly,
"Yes, you bitch", my eyes

shot open, muscles clenched
and I noticed the latticework
dirt lining our bedroom fan.

Afreen Azim

Loveboat

Scalloped edges run
across your velvet skin,
catching eyes, affording just
a little too much, too little.

Fingers, mine,
wanting, wandering,
hesitant.
I trace the fringes
of your body, soul till
our pupils meet, dilate.

Hands reaching, grasping,
Cradling, while your pliant lips
throb, ebb, encompassing
mine and parting in
the epicurean bliss
of this moment's isolation.

Gentle waves tug
this sinking ship deeper,
down into the depths of
our waxen sheets,
rocking you and I
into you.

A shudder,
sigh. A left
breast enclosed so
gently in my loving clasp and
your flowing hair tucked, buried
in the shallow
cove of my chest.

Ignatius Tan

ambient lights watch

steel duvet begging linen rope burn to get off

To My Work

I cannot make love to my work.
I cannot kiss it with my open loving mouth.
I cannot taste my work,
it neglects that sense completely.

I cannot pull my work close and feel its warmth
for minutes, much less hours at a time.
I cannot hold it against me
and get a rise off its arousing scent.

I cannot be held by my work,
like the Venus de Milo, it has no arms!
It stands there and looks back at me for eternity
waiting for me to do everything.
But it is always what it is and not a touch more.

I cannot make my work sweat,
it is always as cool as sliced cucumber
awaiting closed eyes at a spa.
My intensity barely registers as a breeze.

I cannot lick my work,
neither of us would feel a thing,
and eventually this tongue would forget
it had a greater purpose in the savorless body of my world
like ear lobes and nipples and envelopes.

I cannot push my body into my work,
I cannot feel it wrapped tight, wet
around inches of my physical form.

I cannot roll around with my work
like we were rolling down
highland hills of windswept skin,
ready at once for death or ecstasy.

I cannot thirst my tongue inside and around my work.
I cannot suck on its sweetness,
or sip from its lips like they are my own.

I cannot make it moan or make it drip upon my face.
I cannot look into its eyes
amid crashing climax as they dilate,
as we pulse and push and cling
then drop off the cliff into
being, being, being.

I cannot dissolve
in a pool of mutual pleasure with my work.

I cannot make love to my work.

KJ Ink

Pressure Points

We are finding sex in unhealthy places.
Flopping out of the corners of a burned pasta bake.
Trickling down the sticky side of dirty dishes.
You are hoarding kisses like trophies.
I am cumming into shower plugholes.
There are riots in our throats that break
the things we're trying to save
and desperation in our unmade bed.

Carl Sealeaf

Out of the Sheets

Sex got horny one night
and decided to try her luck
in the dictionary.

Her mind was lost
in nervous excitement
as she dreamt
of being bent over a line
break, feeling a sentence
stuff a thick hyphen ins-
-ide her, as she nestled her tongue
in the body of a paragraph.

With the textual undertones
of a preposition,
she propositioned
a palindrome, and some anagrams
for some wordplay so Wilde,
they'd have to punnish her for
coming
without syntax.

But as the stanza ended,
she lay there spent
amidst spilt syllables, still
unsatisfied, waiting
for some rogue bookworm
that would eat her out of the sheets.

Abishek Balasubramanian

Speaking in Tongues

These lips have long been underused.

Years wasted on utterances nowhere near

the landscape of your body, housing a tongue

that knows not of cherry knots but of melted ice

cream on the fleshiest part of my palms. No more.

I will now use them exactly as they are meant for.

Singing psalms to cushion your fall from grace.

Open lips, like fingers, greeting half parted

sighs of gods too shy to peek through.

Sheena Baharudin

daddy issues

last night, I was suspended
from the ceiling by a rope harness,
made to candlewax
lyrical about the progress
our nation has made.
sir told me our safeword could be
paternalism / censorship / welfare.

thank you sir—may I please have another?
thank you sir—may I please have another—

look
at all we've accomplished,
all your foreskinned foresight—

don't you know the judicial caning penalty
only teaches you to clench
your buttocks in fear

when grey berets
gang up on you at crowded
intersections demanding
where's your passport and
what's in your backpack
—but that's only for your own good.

so I sucked it up
like I was already used to enemas,
allowed sir to plug his indoctrination
into my ass

an anal plug shaped
like a remote control,
was told to hold
it—hold
it—hold—

if you work hard enough,

maybe you'll earn the right
to sleep
in a bed tonight

a BTO*,
married life,
housing rights,
safety from racial profiles,
political exiles—

who's a good girl?
who's
a
good girl?

"sir,
I can't hold it anymore.
I think all of my indignation
is leaking
out."

so he told me to be quiet
dribble my anger into the gdp
squatting over a bucket
labelled worker productivity

straining
to boost the economy—

sir controls access to basic commodity
just so you won't be lazy.
maybe if you satisfy sir tonight
you'll be allowed clean water
and food and air.

if you don't like it, then why don't you
just live in some other dungeon?
don't you know compared to other slaves
you're already very spoilt?
don't you need your
strong, first-world dom

to protect you against the big bad
terrorism / marxism / civil unrest /
alternative lifestyles?

do you want to be one of those slaves
whose heads are shaved?
don't you know conscription
is just another humiliation

because if we bond over dick jokes
we might forget we are bending over
in service to the nation,

might forget our testes
are in someone else's
fist.

what do you mean, "is this blindfold necessary?"
it's not like you ever see anything
I don't want you to see.

why don't you vote me back into office
so you can crawl back between my legs
and tell me how much you like it
under my desk?

daddy's happy that you're happy.
I mean, it makes you happy daddy's happy.
I mean, daddy's happy that
you're happy that he's happy.
I mean, if you're not happy
we can talk about it

but first
put on this ball gag.

Marylyn Tan

*Built-To-Order, a Housing & Development Board flat allocation system that makes it
  difficult to obtain government housing for Singaporeans under 35 who are not able to
  or decide not to get married.

Jouir

Just the tip.
Just to see
what it feels like.

Just to trust
the tendril
of a trailing

tremor, delicately
through some
sacred place.

By through I
mean passing.

By passing I
mean passage.

I mean a precisely
prosed perch.

A precipice
and a slip—

Tongue, dance,
doom or desire,

In me there
moves an
other

spilling like
a sound

sliding
into fire.

Samuel Caleb Wee

Cam Flesh

return to primal nudity
a bodiless sundress on fire
lace, ashen, burnt

black bra hung
on spine of chair
where she sits erect
(flash)

so china white (flesh)

      "Writhe for me."

every flash on flesh
whitens my weekly-hourly bride
photographs strung on
thin laundry rope,
metal clothes-pins, pinching
white turning red

photos of bodies on beds
place her headshot on shaven snatch
(flash)

smack
slap
(flash)
smack smoking, dragon girl, never to dull
shame or pain but

"I want to drift in your dream."

      "Come."

sprawling so lazy
half dazed cat stretched on
sweaty mattress

stretch marks, surgical
stitches on belly

close up (flash)

"Used to be my baby."

(flash)

close up, burnt hole
cigarette smoke, eyes glazed
role (to) play, fighting
hurting
cowering

"Love is a mess, all noise and pain."

my drowsy seducee
(hourly, fortnightly)

        "Don't smile, (flash)
        look, you're sad, see
        (flash) soot on your cheek, yes
        good, hurt a little
        yes. (flash) wet
        cheeks, yes, see."
        (flash)

white thong between teeth

        "Are you hungry?"

"No."
never eats
skin and bones
starved and sexual
spine curved
tingling
so thin, oh

        "Suck in your tummy, yes."

rib, cage
prisoner
laundry rope marks
don't smile
(flash)

"Who owns you?" (flash)

"Master."

a little bruise here,
            there,
            the corner of lips, slight
bleed
bite marks of the beast
blue
black
red
slash

"Are we sick?"

"No."

"Skin and shadow and needle marks.
Other holes in familiar bodies."
"Who are we to judge? Can we?"

"No."

"Pan* made pain. God made the sick."

"From dark came light."

"Yes."
"Love is a sickness. Love is a medicine."
codeine, valium,
heroine. My heroine."

"Yes?" (flash)

"They like it. God made them.
Made us." (flash)

"He loves us?"

"Yes."

"She loves you."
she smiles

"One hour."

"Yes."

"Pay."

"Yes."

Irving Paul Pereira

*In Greek religion and mythology, Pan is famous for his sexual powers and is often depicted with a phallus.

Epididymis

to tear skin from foreskin:
the soul aches to moult every time
it happens.

to split soul from the body, spurt
by long spurt, desperate
to escape the immolating abode.

suddenly, I am
but my body's leakage, spilled
broken across

a stranger's bedroom floor
while it retrieves itself,
showers and leaves.

Ang Ming Wei

Doorbell

Here we are, reeling from the audacity
of occupying a room together, our bodies
abandoned at my bedframe as if
waiting to be noticed or collected,
tongues toiling assiduously
at ice cream and conversation. I am not
permitted this clemency, even as you
begin to conquer the rift
echoing between us. Your arm
is not warming my shoulder,
our noses not understanding odours
for the first time. When your face takes mine
in like walls to silence, it is not an excuse
to crave. How long can proximity
deny dependence? This is a room of
too many omens: tap water idling
in a mug, sun locked away by curtains,
your shirt collapsed on the carpet
like a means to an end. Yet if familiarity
is what it takes for you to be here,
your lips persevering in
its gentle craft, its whispers
roaring across the infinite dormant
caves of my body, so be it. There will
be fresh sheets when you call.

Jerrold Yam

Five.

In the throw pillow fortress,

a spinning wheel turns

silk into dragons.

Gods We Are

Once, I taught a parrot to say *fuck*.
The neighbours complained.
Called the bird vulgar.
Obscene.
Inappropriate.
Never bothered to learn the parrot's name.
(it was Molly)
They were only concerned
with how this bird made god spoke
new life into their private worlds.

We talk like we are our own gods.
Speaking the world into existence.
Speaking desires into our lives.
Call it love.
Call it right.
One does not exist without a name.
But I know you exist,
because I call your name into my bed every night.

Jedidiah Huang

Di Bukit Larangan[*]

(for H.)

those gentle lovers: with their hair pulled (gently), fingers traveling
light distance, perspiration pooling beneath breasts and bellies, within
the rims of their socks, wilted, worn, long forgotten—

you would think they'd be more aware of their feet creating
cacophanies so interruptive of slumber. i stay still, buried
within uphill loam, my body sinking when theirs rise,
and will rise

again in the morning, three hours from now, when the sands of night
are brushed from their eyes. perhaps they do not remember this place
is a giant gravestone, a collective of the ghosts of succession; once a
man came here and built his house, proud. another time

the cannons stood majestically facing the wrong way. upon these
grounds the washed up men gave their red faces the reign of japanese.
bricks and mortar have been put up only to be brought down again.
with these steps upon my head so insistent, perhaps these lovers will
see the dawn

crashing.

Benedicta J. Foo

---

*Di Bukit Larangan is a Malay phrase which means 'at Forbidden Hill'. It is the former
name of Fort Canning Hill, Singapore.

Behind Telegraph Avenue[*]

This year, Saint Patrick's Day fell on a humid weekend.
From the bathroom, Benoit could see a row of clothing shops.
Benoit stepped out of the shower with only a tea towel.
His upper body was a large square, his legs well-built.
His neck and arms were sturdy and thick, with a light tan.
His was a natural physique, effortless, the smell of country.
He looked at Baptiste, who was still dressed, a yard from the bed.
And beside Baptiste, three Korean tourists giggling, looking away.
The three women held their evening purses close to them.
By the couch was a tray table, and on it, various oval dishes.
Bread pudding with a bowl of vanilla and caramel on the side.
A hunky cut of meat, a chateaubriand steak, just seared.
Dribbled over it was a béarnaise sauce, a wedge of butter on top.
The flask of red wine seemed vulgar without other glassware.
Baptiste dipped a finger into the butter, brought it to his lips.
He took the glistening yellow to Benoit's right nipple.
Then a spot of vanilla to draw a circle around Benoit's left nipple.
Benoit merely stood in the same place, surprised but calm.
The three women had stopped their giggles, watching quietly.
Baptise took Benoit's large hands, the towel dropped to the floor.
It was wet, a puddle at Benoit's feet, wet like his calves and thighs.
Baptiste brought his tongue to the butter, then the vanilla.
He used his forefinger to take a bit of the taste from his mouth.
Then parted Benoit's lips with his finger, to taste the same.
By now, Benoit's hands were trembling, held close to his thighs.
He knew he would have Baptiste tonight, have him to himself.
Even if it was in front of these strangers, by now seated on chairs.
The chairs were made of solid oak, with embroidered seats.
The backrests rose like small walls, lacquered pattern of songbirds.
And a phoenix and falcon above the trees, in a dance to the dawn.

Desmond Kon Zhicheng-Mingdé

[*]Telegraph Avenue is a street in the historical downtown district of Oakland, California. A site of numerous protests and riots since the 1960s, it is home to many Korean-owned restaurants, bookstores and clothing shops.

Pondering a Kernel of Corn

Jealousy trickles under
the fleshed door of my existence,
as I marvel at the power
of self-mutation—
like mutilation but prettier
—the ability to rip
its insides wholly out
like the inspired shell
of a shotgun.

Gripped in my palm
like a firecracker, quietly
I hope it will peel back
layers of my being
with its disturbing potential
—separate cartilage
from its god-given bone—,
so I will feel as though
I were shaking
hands with an atomic
change.

The inexplicable nature
of this compressed energy
is like a heart born
with a single swelling beat:
A percussion that will ignite,
like lightning to sand,
into a sensuous shape
of love.

This is what time truly is: a moment
when a glob of hydrogen and oxygen explodes
into frozen fleeting symmetry.
I long to live in that moment's lovely house
and be next-door neighbors
with corpses and newborns;

where I can storm into the backyard
and constantly break new ground
by shoving a shovel into the dust-
filled brain matter of the world
and be like the first poet who thought:

"I will not stick one word next to the other like graves
as all the dead poets did

              I want   to see
the   word s
             floating
                    in the white lake

    of   the page

            like   scattered

     ashes."

KJ Ink

Ishtar by Moonlight

Ishtar* by moonlight we lie at your gate,
receive us tonight, drink us dry, we pray.
When the pits of your longing beckon
the meek lambs of Judah,
myths are truer things.

Ishtar by moonlight your mammaries are runes.
You know I have seen it. These ovaries are ruins.
I have seen the fertility figures gorging on the world
as the bony bodies of our memories starve,
as we run from seraphims and hide in the dirt
as we burrow into coffins and take off our shirts
as we sleep with the calcified counting up the wake
at which only pixels rise at your name. Stop,
and think of that.

So warmly, Ishtar, when your riverbank thighs
brings me to boiling at hotsong and croon,
in a milky incandescent birth
I turn like the tail of Tiamat†. First
the little one, then the cold death,
but eventually the stars lap into rest.
I see a bad sun dissipating like smoke.
I look back to gather salt for dead seas.
In an amniotic lake, a salmon spurts upstream.
Floating on my back, I try
to interpret clouds, but
see only sky, seeded
by lone moon.

Samuel Caleb Wee

*An ancient Babylonian deity of fertility and sex. A famous part of her myth describes
her descent to the underworld through the seven gates of hell, shedding one item of
clothing as she did so, until she was finally naked.

†The primordial Babylonian serpent of the ocean; she is simultaneously the deity of
creation as well as chaos. After she and her husband were killed in an uprising by the
new gods, her body formed the heavens, and her tail became the Milky Way.

Bedcide Museum in ##sections##

##sex&death##
(installations at the body farm)
-traditional crucifixion †
-reverse prayer position
-metamorphosis of the monarch
-the star X
-neptune's bride (with octopi, eels)

##paragon of implements##
(furniture constructs made from pipe, iron bars and planks)
-ice picks, spikes
-plastic bags
-fire brand
-wooden stake
-cattle prod
-iron maiden

##aquariums with figures##
(wax replicas)
-fresh period blood on skin (such an art form)
-let tongue dangle (honey drip)
-baby talcum (slipping between the cracks)
-soil, venus fly traps (vines)
-live (serpents)

#film series#
(exploration of extreme emotional states)
-ice
-sweatbox intercourse
-gentlemen on pure bred stallions sporting rifles
 in heat of hunt (nude fox runs blind in dense fields)
-electrical wire wound, copper currents (skin sweat wet)
-premature burial with sexual devices attached (12-hour director's cut)

#medical hall#
(speculum & investigation of body orifices)
-implementation and removal of vaginal sutures
-artificial limbs
-bandage bondage
-oxygen deprivation
-acupuncture
-enema

*human toilet available upon request
**no entry for minors

Irving Paul Pereira

Bedsheets

The dog has vomited more times than I
from meat too large to swallow,
is what Deep Throat the Bedsheet
would tell you if she spoke.

The watergates would spill of arched backs
      Hands sliding under
A cupful of flesh
      Tender, gentle
Lips
      Smack
Wet stains
      Stifled screams
Cotton-filled mouths
      Thumped fists

She will show you the art
of restraining wrists, to knot
around feet, be bundled as prop
for all the right angles.

When you ask of her favourite positions,
she will answer that they change
with the curve of your neck, the pressure
of teeth on skin.

She will trace fingers along heaving breath,
ask to meet your bedsheets to share the same bed;
discover what tingles your skin.

I keep her away in case she lets slip
the way I hold her around my body,
her arms as yours.
Falling asleep with the wonder
of what your bedsheets would say
if you let them speak.

Charlene Shepherdson

About the Contributors

When *Abishek Balasubramanian* is not pretending to write poetry, make puns, or be meta, he's busy thinking about the implications of writing one's own bio in third person.

Ang Ming Wei is a full time national serviceman and writes poetry as a hobby. He won a merit prize at the inaugural National Poetry Competition (2015). His poems can also be found on the online literature and art journal *We Are A Website*, and *SingPoWriMo 15: The Anthology*.

Afreen Azim is a 26 year old aspiring poet and academic. She is currently working on a PhD proposal while doing volunteer work with an activist group.

Benedicta J. Foo is an aspiring writer who seeks comfort in the moon and its tides. Her poem 'Between Here' has been awarded a Certificate of Merit in Singapore's inaugural National Poetry Festival.

Christopher Fok works with the architecture of stories, for everything of note is made of them; brands, spaces, people. He believes that a strong narrative architecture ensures a lasting quality, a building you go back to again and again, just to look at the arches.

Carl Sealeaf is a spoken word artist and problem solver. He's been writing all his life, but stumbled face-first into spoken word about 5 years ago and is still trying to find his way out. Carl is co-founder of Pangaea Poetry, a group of spoken word artists around the world using digital technology to bring poetry to more people. Collectively, they're responsible for digital troublemaking such as the Pangaea Poetry Slam and Converse/Converge—a 24 hour online conference/festival of spoken word.

Desmond Kon Zhicheng-Mingdé is the author of an epistolary novel, a hybrid work, and 5 poetry collections. Poetry editor at Kitaab.org, he has also edited more than 15 books and co-produced 3 audio books. An interdisciplinary artist, Desmond helms Squircle Line Press as its founding editor.

Drima Chakraborty is a literature major at National University of Singapore and was a dubious virgin with a strong imagination when they wrote these poems. They like black cats, black lipsticks, black leather harnesses and green tea, and can be found doing strange things (less strange than their kinks) at @drimachuck on Twitter.

Ignatius Tan began writing poetry between pints of Asahi and (not) studying for his A-levels, realizing a childhood dream that he had previously shelved. His current responsibilities in National Service, when he isn't on medical leave, have done nothing to deaden his love for the language. He hopes to one day publish his own collection of poetry.

Irving Paul Pereira is a B.D.S.M enthusiast and an absurd garden that grows strange visual phenomena and oneiric literature. Observations can be made at ipaulpereira.com.

Jason Purdy is a writer and digital marketer. He writes poems, short stories, novels that will never be published, and pointless words about video games. In his free time, he likes to go to the gym, and try to force his cat and girlfriend to love him.

Jedidiah Huang is a full-time national serviceman. He graduated from Catholic Junior College, and intends to further his studies at the National University of Singapore. While he has managed to survive twenty years (and counting) without a broken bone, he is not as prudent with his heart. This is also why he writes poetry.

Jerrold Yam (b. 1991) is a lawyer and the author of three poetry collections: *Intruder* (2014), *Scattered Vertebrae* (2013) and *Chasing Curtained Suns* (2012). He has received poetry awards from the British Council, National University of Singapore and Poetry Book Society, and been nominated for the Forward and Pushcart Prizes. He is named by the National Arts Council as one of the "New Voices of Singapore 2014".

Keith Tong is a student and an aspiring poet. His work has been published in *A Luxury We Cannot Afford, SingPoWriMo 2014: The Anthology, From Walden to Woodlands*, and he has performed for Singapore Writers Festival 2014. When he is bored, he wanders around IKEA and tries out all the furniture. Drawing strength from a diet of coffee and chocolate, he runs and dances in his spare time.

KJ Ink has been bouncing between writing, teaching and performing poetry for the past 5 years. After 15 years of quiet writing and 10 years of patient teaching led him realize he could do more. He could embody his words. He could not take so much for granted.

Marylyn Tan is a full-time linguistics major and part-time cuddle fiend who has been featured in SPORE Art Salon, IndigNation SG, Lit Up 2015, SPEAK., Singapore Writers Festival, and various print and online anthologies. She has been called an 'erotic poet', and writes for your bewilderment. Her natural habitat: mrylyn.wordpress.com

Nickie Jamison enjoys a good spanking. Her short erotic fiction has been published in the *Coming Together Among the Stars, Coming Together Outside the Box,* and *Slice Girls* anthologies. Nickie's hobbies include knitting and binge watching Netflix. She lives in Hampton Roads with her husband and furbabies, Jayne and Frye.

Pamela Ng is passionate about and actively engaged in the arts and social causes. This has seen her managing fine art galleries and curating art exhibitions. She has published her poetry in First Words and exhibited her poetry with her iPhone photography in group shows such as Nostra 2 and rememberingLKY.

Rodrigo Dela Peña, Jr. is the author of the chapbook *Requiem*. His poems have been published in *Quarterly Literary Review Singapore, We are a Website, Hayden's Ferry Review* and anthologies such as *A Luxury We Cannot Afford* and *From Walden to Woodlands*. He is a recipient of the Palanca Award for Poetry in the Philippines, as well as numerous awards from British Council Singapore's Writing the City.

As a poet and a journalist, *Samuel Caleb Wee*'s work has appeared in a number of publications such as Facebook, Tumblr and Twitter. Due to his commitment to facilitating subaltern expression in the local literary scene, Samuel voluntarily runs a creative writing workshop for community cats on weekends.

See Wern Hao is a writer, prospective law student and frequent debtor to the National Library Board for overdue book fines. He is a member of the writing collective Burn After Reading and his poetry is featured in the anthology *A Luxury We Must Afford*.

Sheena Baharudin is a poet-educator, travel & lifestyle writer and author of *Rhymes for Mending Hearts* (2013). She is the founder of Numinous, the KL-based gig which has since featured more than a hundred local and international artists. Her second book of poems is scheduled for publication in early 2016.

Stephanie Chan has won national poetry slams in Singapore (2010) and the UK (2012) and has performed in 10 different countries. Her writing is published in the *Asian Literary Review, Quarterly Literary Review Singapore* and *Body Boundaries: The EtiquetteSG Anthologies*. She is part of the feminist spoken word collective Sekaliwags.

About the Editors

Charlene Shepherdson is interested in the intersection where environment, heritage and technology meet. She has been published in anthologies by Math Paper Press and Ethos Books, featured in open mics in Asia and exhibited her visual text in the Arts House, the Substation and in Singapore libraries under National Art Council's Project LAVA.

Using language in written, performative and visual forms to bridge communities and empower voices, her current research spans narrative design in serious games, interactive art and stories, and creative arts therapy. She is also 1/3 of the spacer.gif collective who run destination: INK, the open-open mic, and a founding member of spoken word troupe Party Action People.

Muslim Sahib wanted to be a porn star but God didn't make him good-looking enough, so he decided to be a poet instead. He performs regularly at open mics and festivals such as destination: INK, Lit-Up Indie Arts Festival and Singapore Writers Festival. He is also the LGBTQ editor for *SimplySxy*, a publication that promotes positive views on sex and sexuality. Muslim is a member Indignation Queer Films which is a non-profit organization that aims to bring Asian queer films to Singapore. Check out his works at sahibtorun.com and simplysxy.com.